LIVELY MANDOLIN TUNES

TOMMY NORRIS

To access the online audio recording go to:

WWW.MELBAY.COM/30816MEB

© 2020 BY MEL BAY PUBLICATIONS, INC.
ALL RIGHTS RESERVED. INTERNATIONAL COPYRIGHT SECURED. MADE AND PRINTED IN U.S.A.
No part of this publication may be reproduced in whole or in part, or stored in a retrieval system, or transmitted in any form
or by any means, electronic, mechanical, photocopying, recording, or otherwise, without written permission of the publisher.

Visit us at www.melbay.com — E-mail us at email@melbay.com

Preface

This is a collection of 38 lively, up-tempo tunes that I've had the pleasure to arrange for mandolin. Backup chords and tablature are included. There are a variety of different styles in this book, including fiddle tunes, reels, hornpipes, jigs, sea chanteys, bluegrass and old-time melodies and some original compositions by William Bay. Each song has a companion recording featuring mandolin with guitar accompaniment. So grab your mandolin, sit back and enjoy learning these timeless and new melodies. I hope you will have as much fun playing these tunes as I had arranging them!

Index of Tunes

Title	Page	Audio Track
American Hornpipe	51	38
Bill Cheathum	4	1
Billy in the Lowground	5	2
Black and White Rag	10	6
Blanchard's Hornpipe	25	15
Bottom of the Punch Bowl Hornpipe	26	16
Brunswick Dance	28	18
Cape Cod Reel	29	19
Catawissa Reel	31	21
Cold, Frosty Morning	6	3
Devil's Dream	32	22
Dixie Breakdown	20	11
East Tennessee Blues	12	7
Echo Canyon	30	20
Haste to the Wedding	33	23
Haul Away, Joe	34	24
Hens in the Kitchen	38	26
High Barbaree	40	28
Hooker's Hornpipe	39	27
Indian Creek	27	17
Jacks Fork Rendezvous	24	14
Katie Trail	42	29
Lady's Fancy	36	25
League Reel	8	5
London Hornpipe	43	30
Lonesome River	45	32
Lost Indian	22	12
Maddie's Bonnet	44	31
Martha's Cider	46	33
Powder Mill	50	37
Rickett's Hornpipe	48	35
Ships are Sailing Reel	47	34
Silver Bell	14	8
Soppin' the Gravy	7	4
Stone's Rag	16	9
Sugar in the Gourd	23	13
Sweet Lillie	18	10
The Wild Mare	49	36

Bill Cheathum

Billy in the Lowground

Cold, Frosty Morning

Brisk Tempo ♩=98

American Fiddle Tune

Soppin' the Gravy

Bluegrass Swing ♩ = 90

League Reel

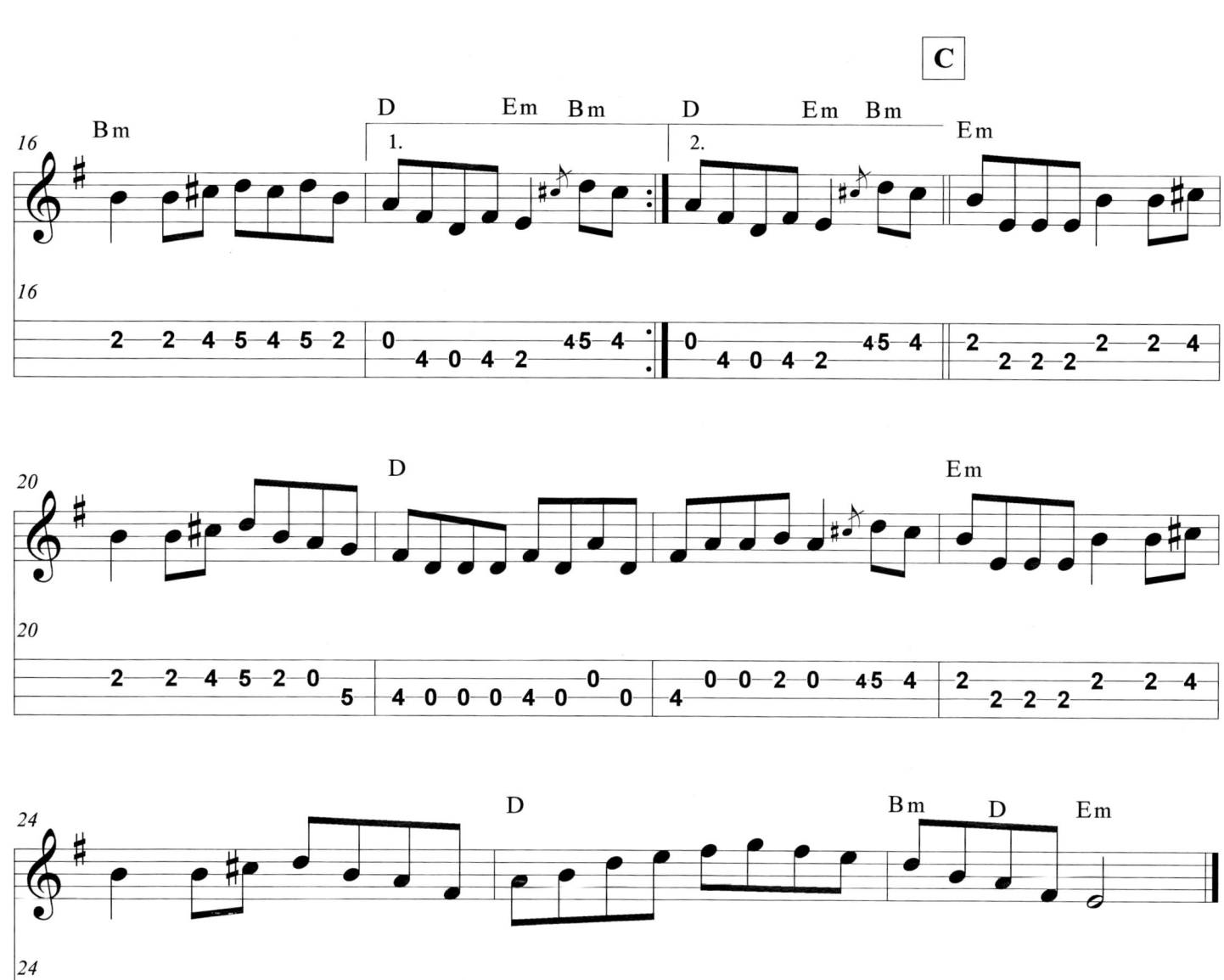

Black and White Rag

Ragtime Swing ♩ = 80 **A**

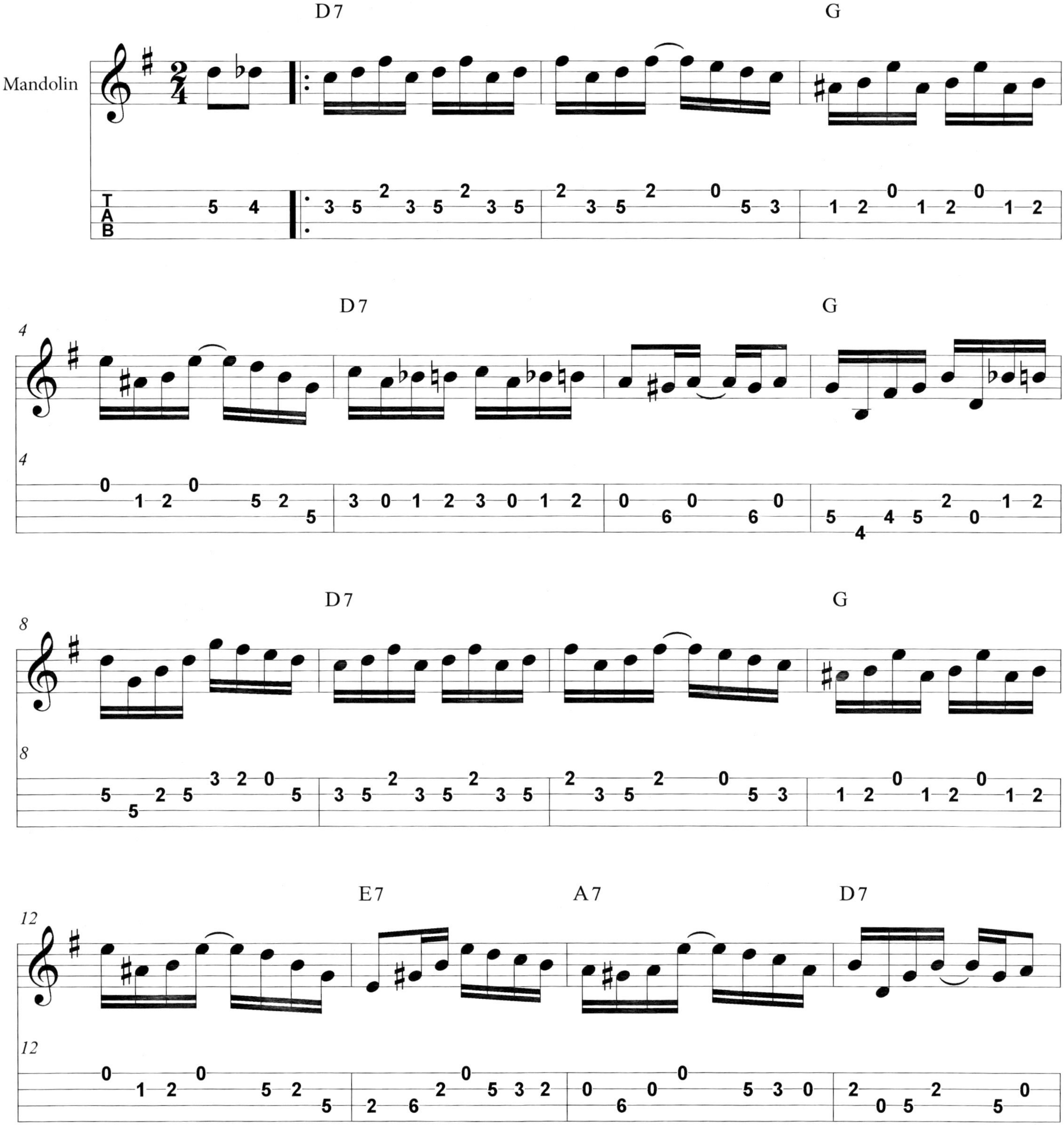

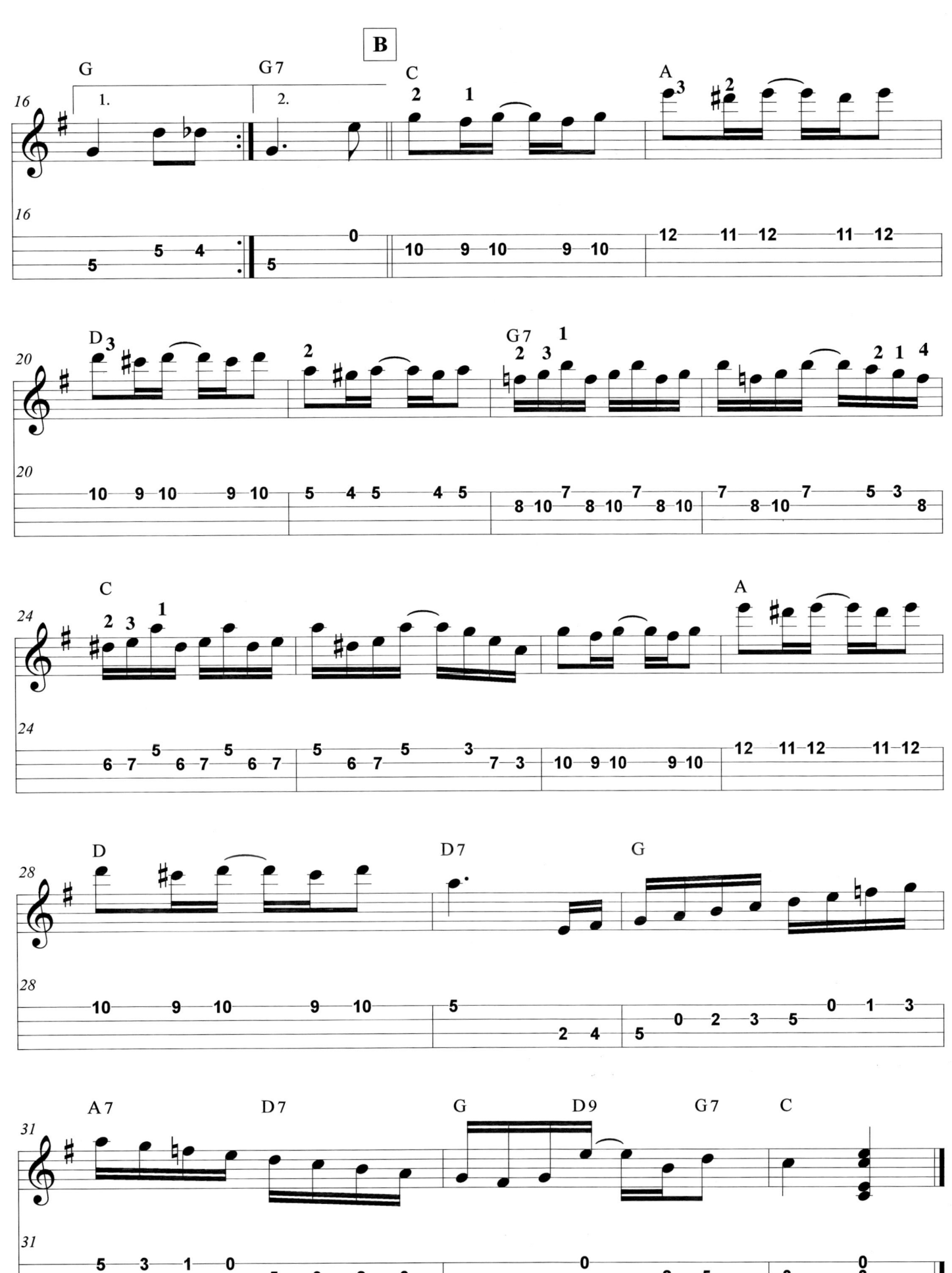

East Tennessee Blues

Medium Swing ♩ = 146

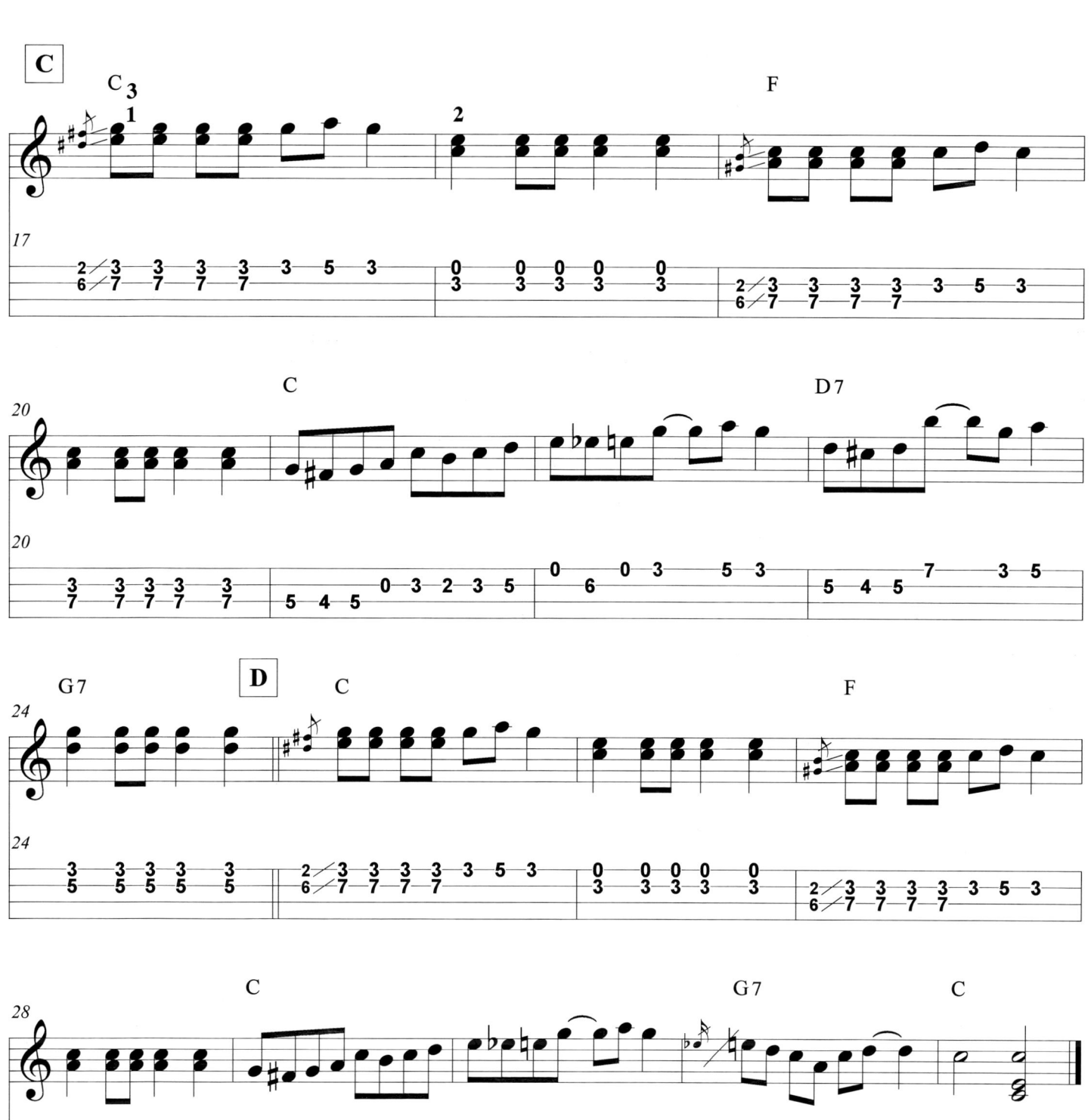

Silver Bell

Stone's Rag

Swing Feeling ♩ = 160

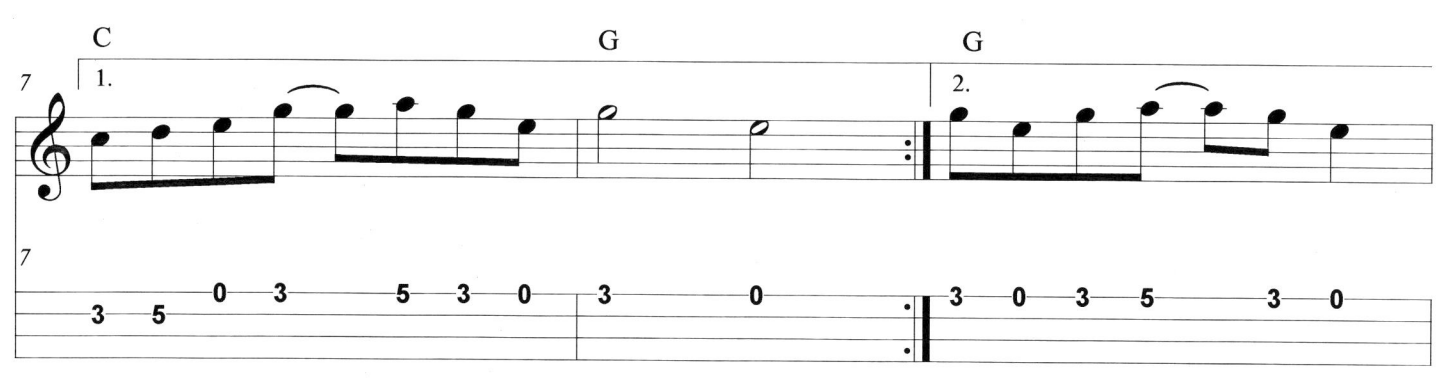

Sweet Lillie

Moderate Tempo ♩ = 88

Appalachian Folk Melody

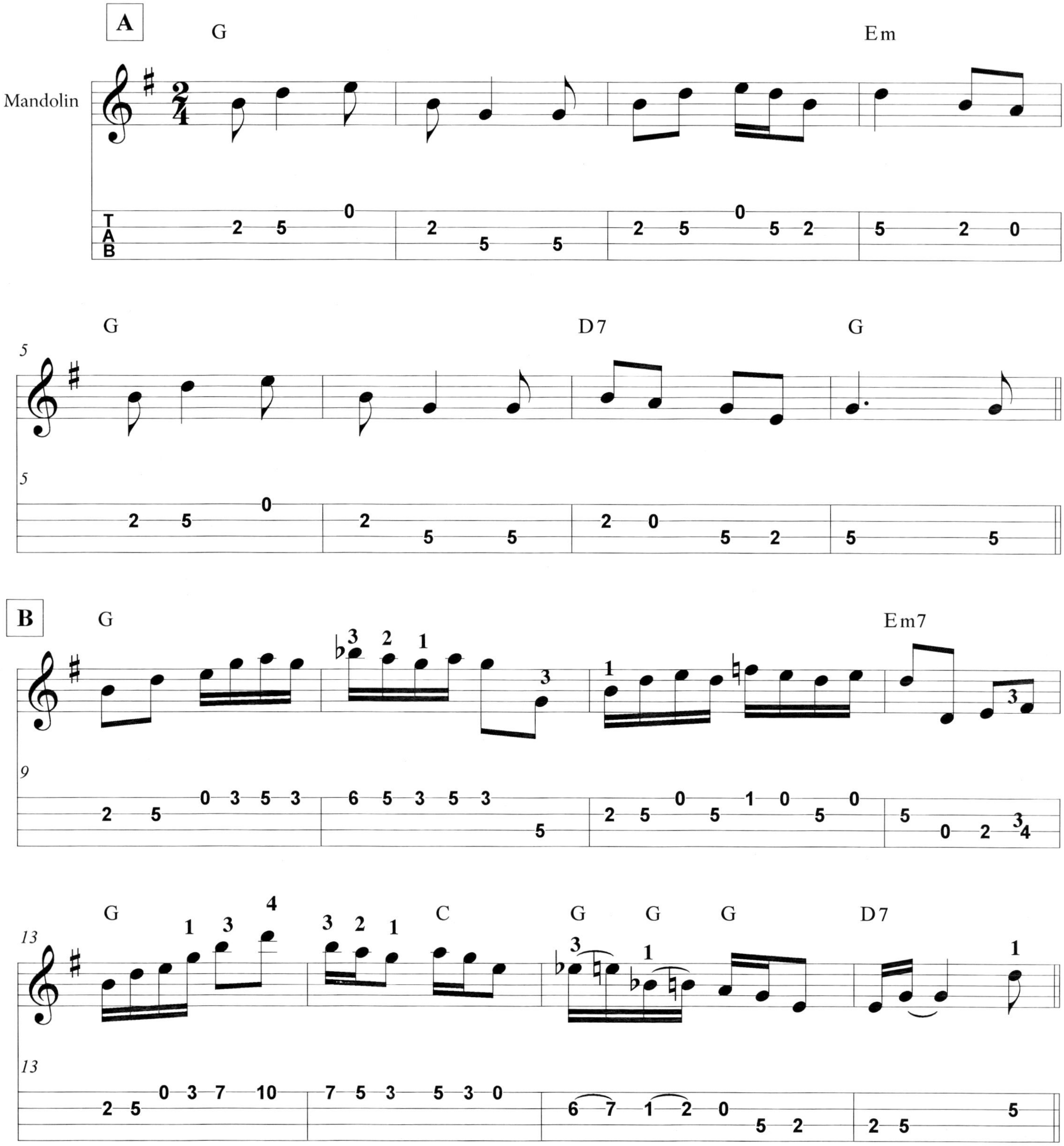

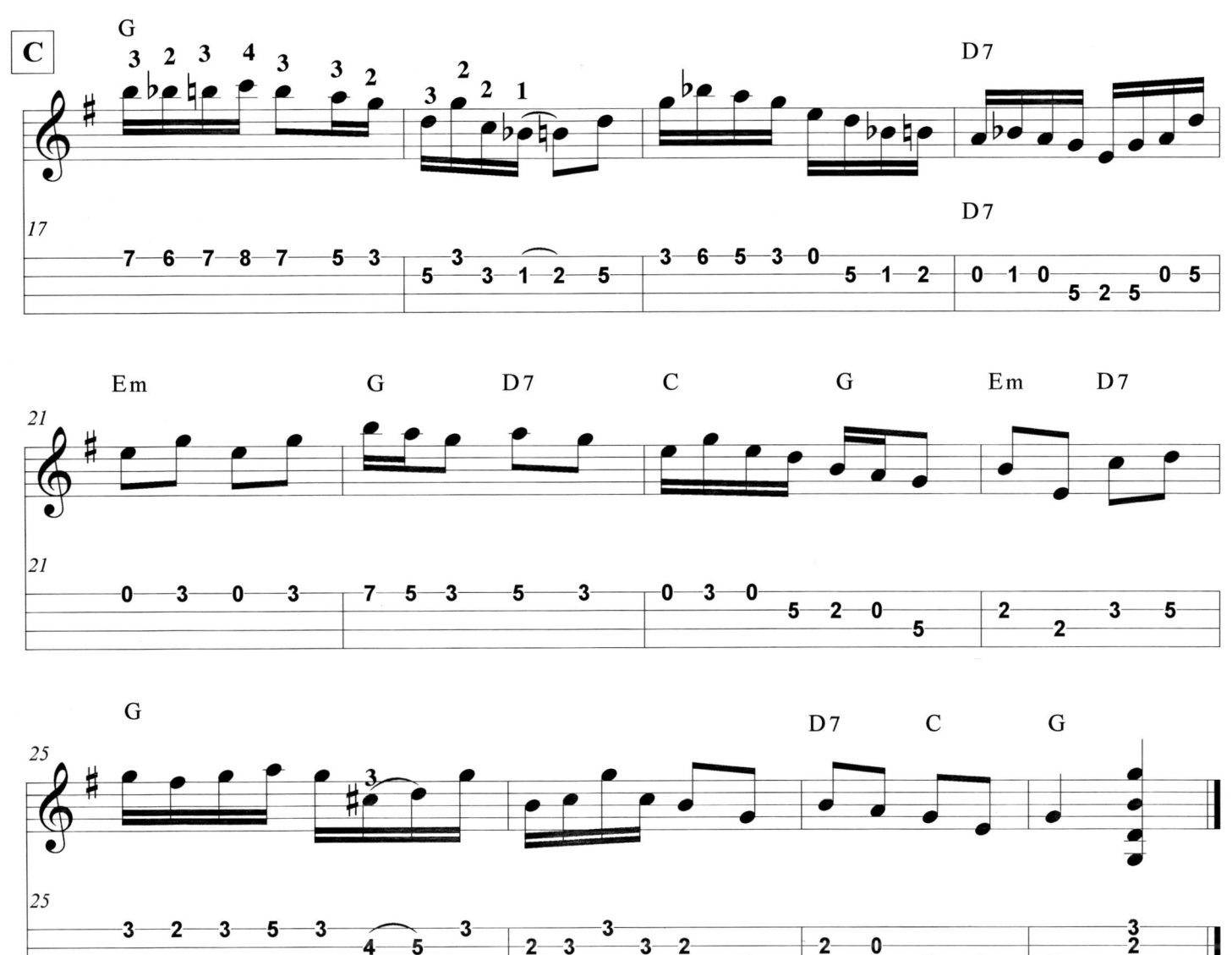

Dixie Breakdown

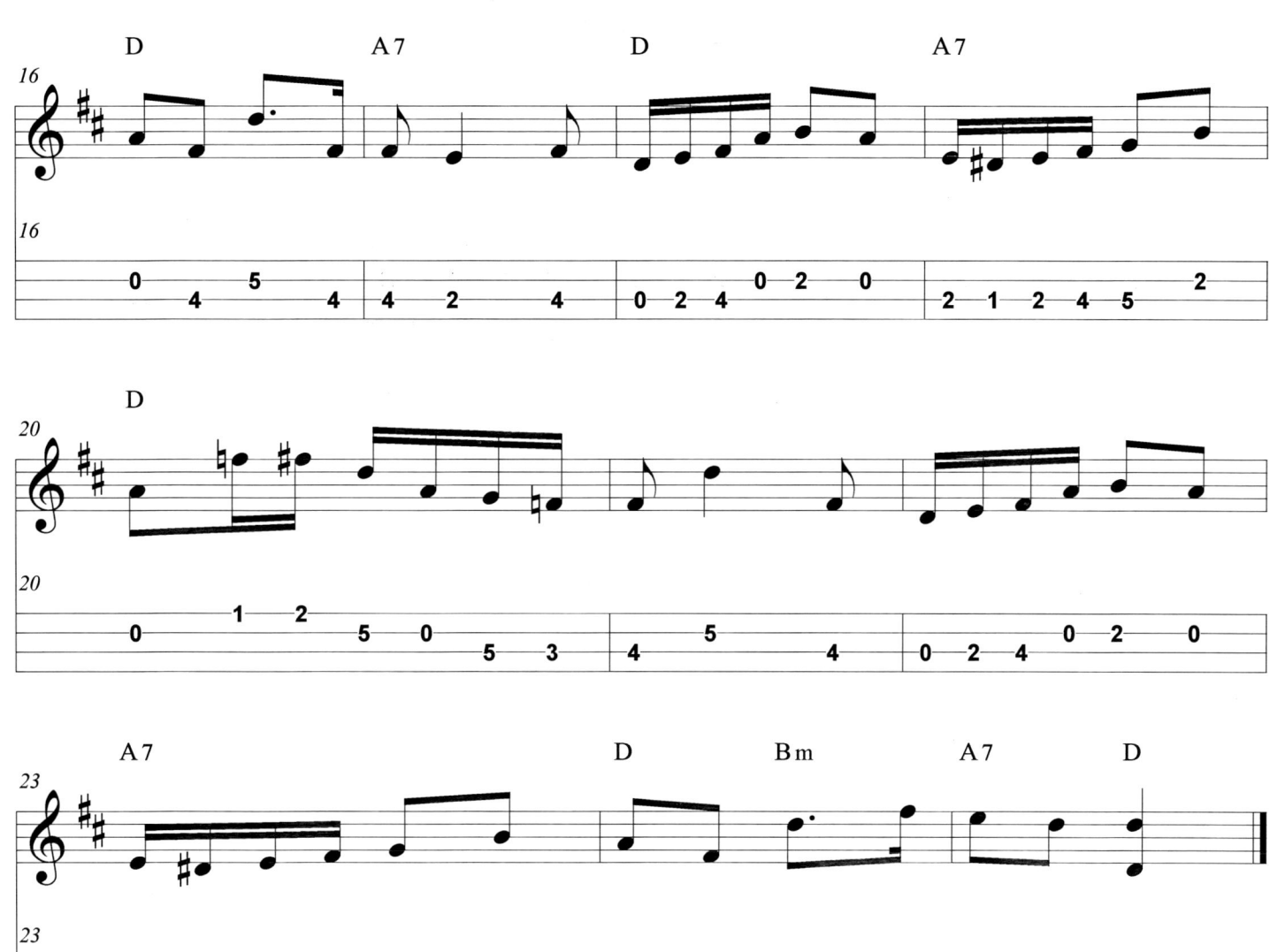

Lost Indian

Bluegrass Swing Tempo ♩= 88

American Fiddle Tune

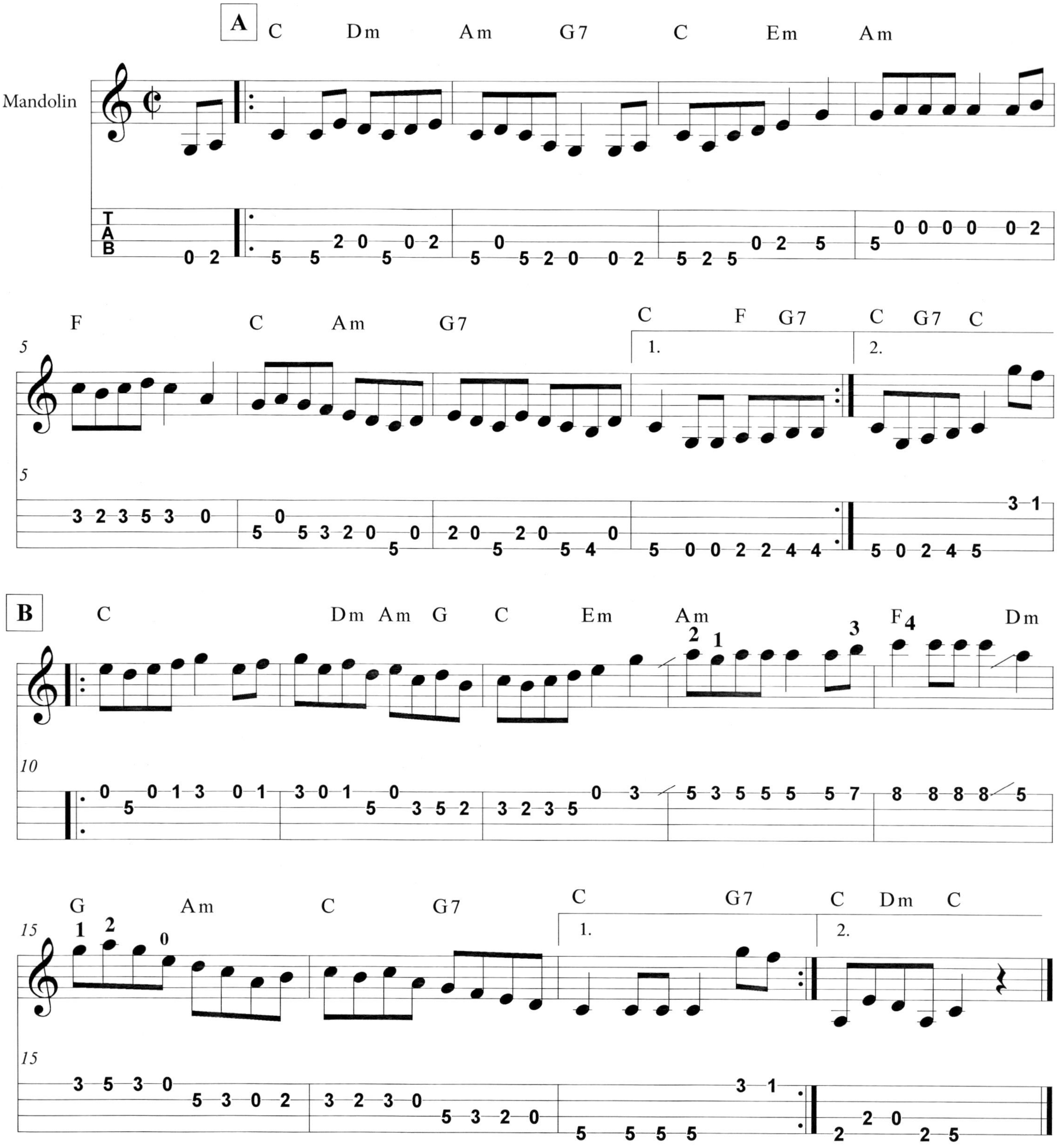

Sugar in the Gourd

Lively Tempo ♩ = 162

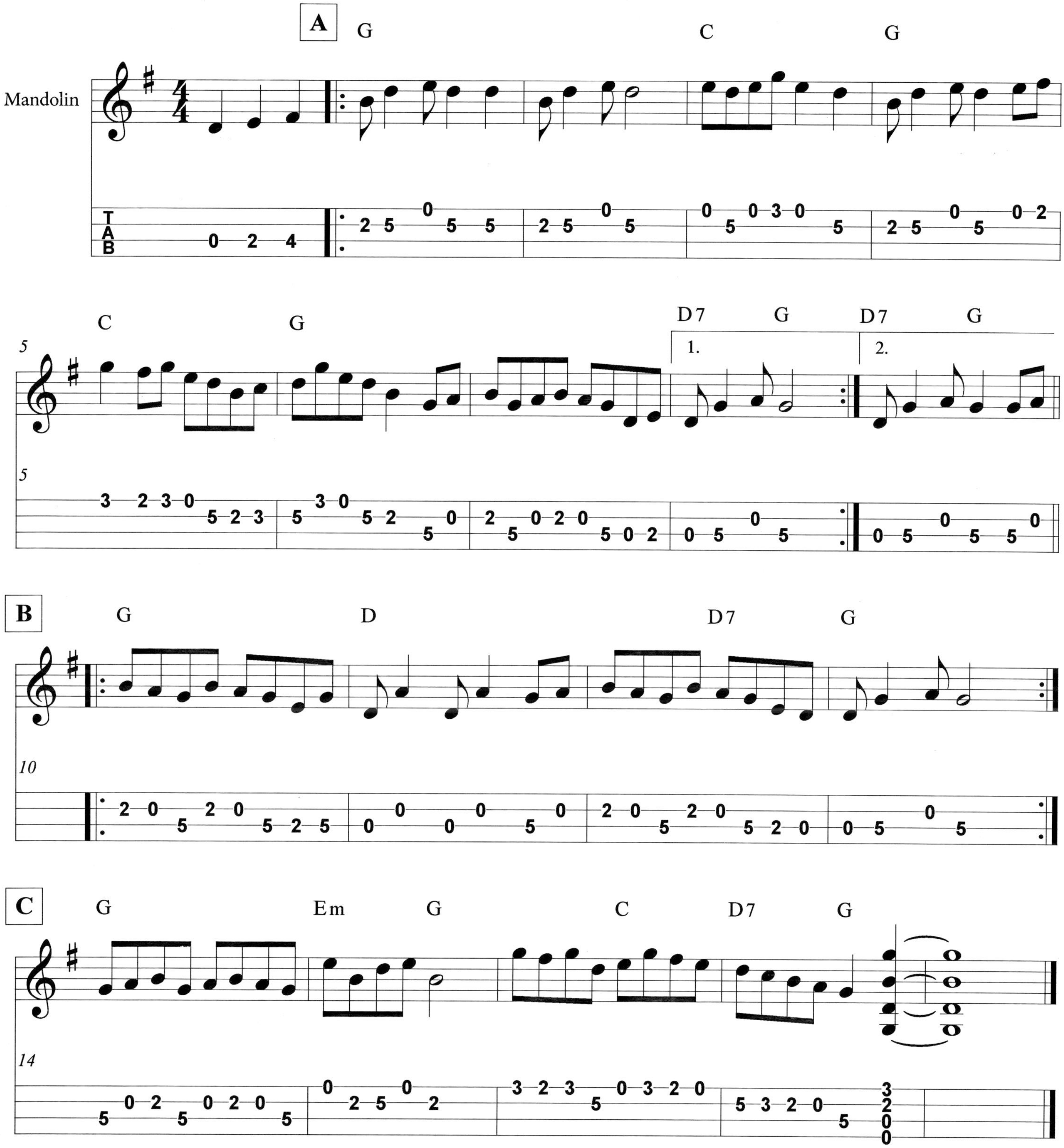

Jacks Fork Rendezvous

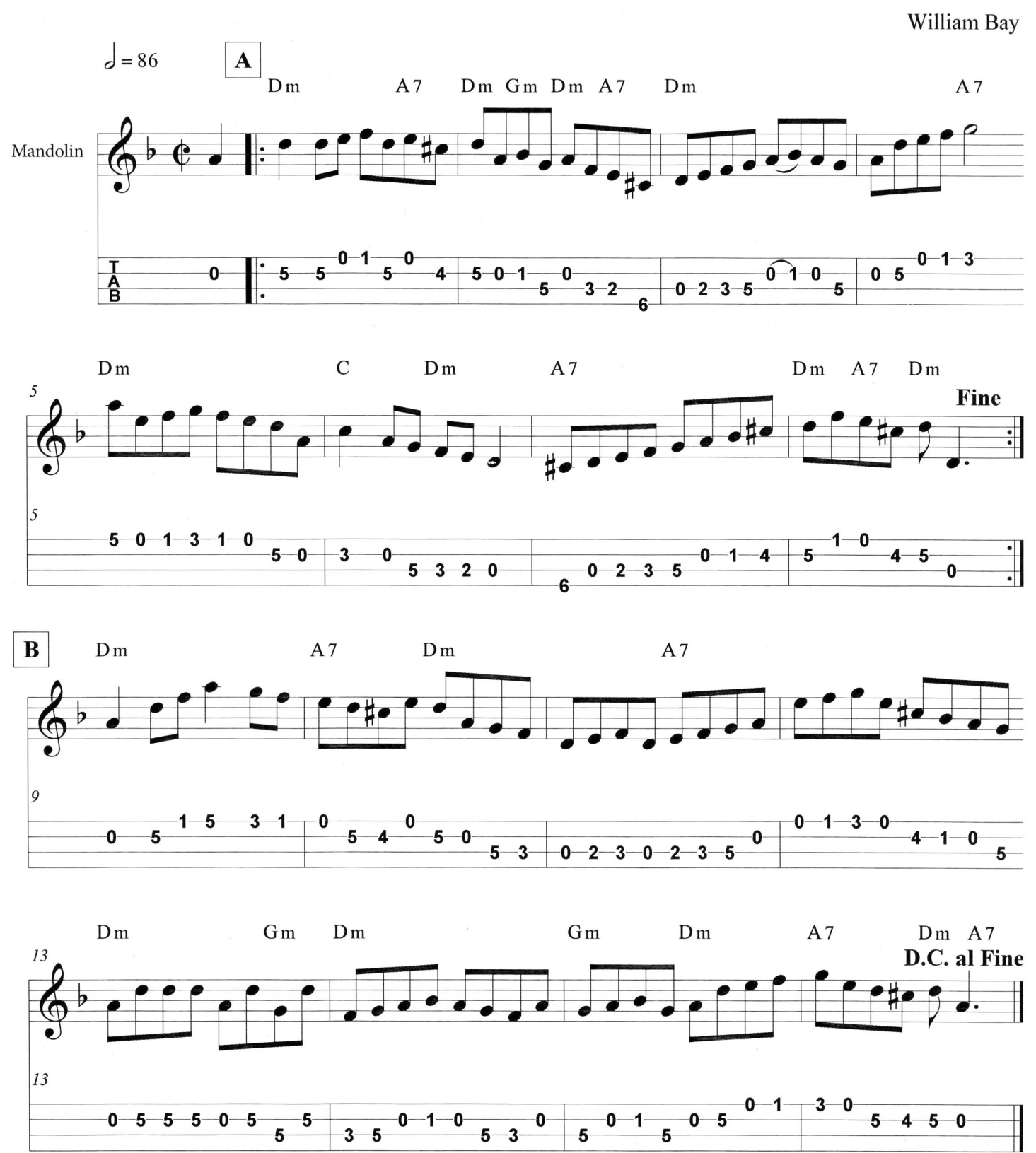

Blanchard's Hornpipe

Bottom of the Punch Bowl Hornpipe

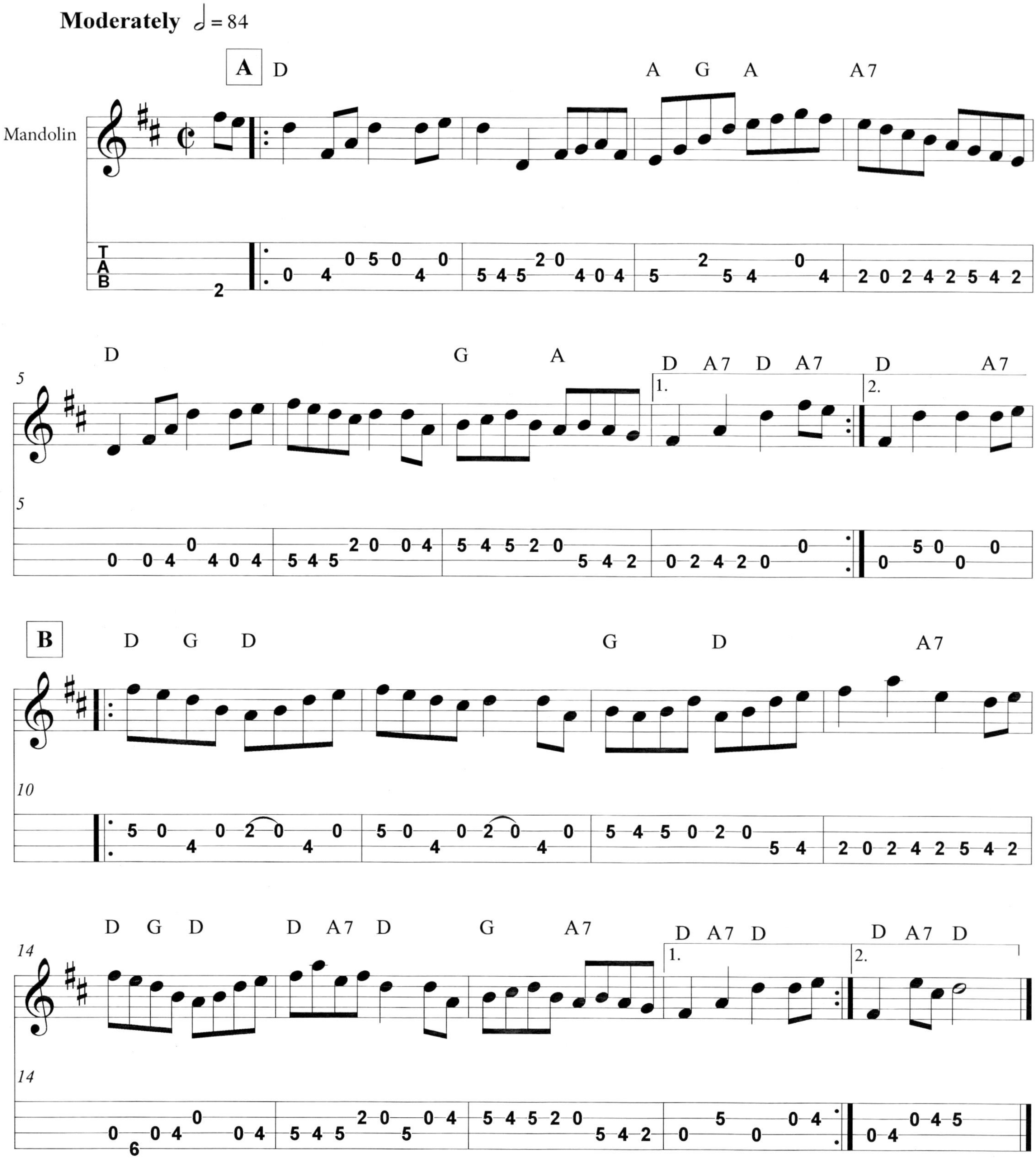

Indian Creek

Brunswick Dance

William Bay

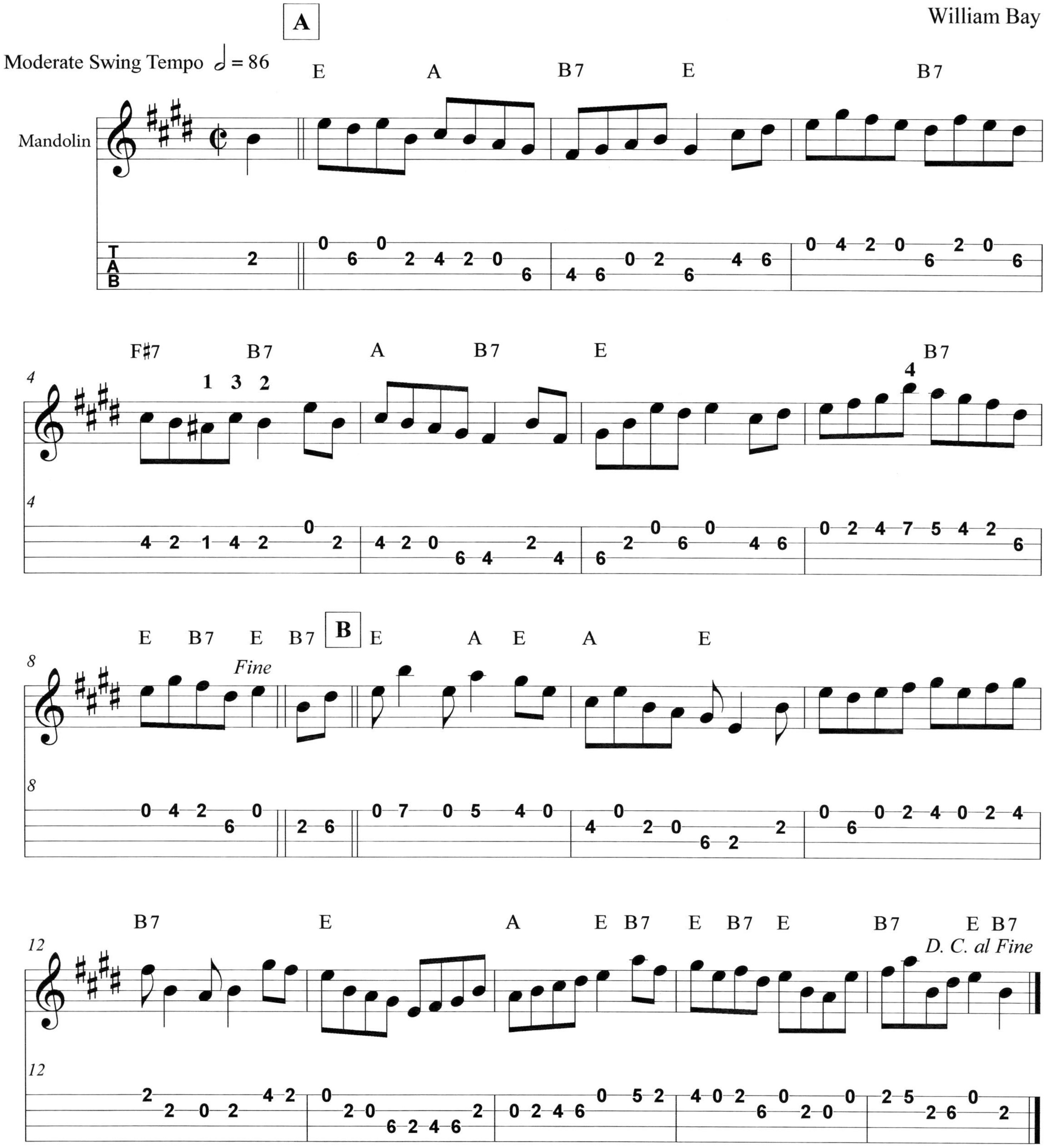

Cape Cod Reel

Echo Canyon

Catawissa Reel

William Bay

Devil's Dream

Lively Tempo ♩ = 88

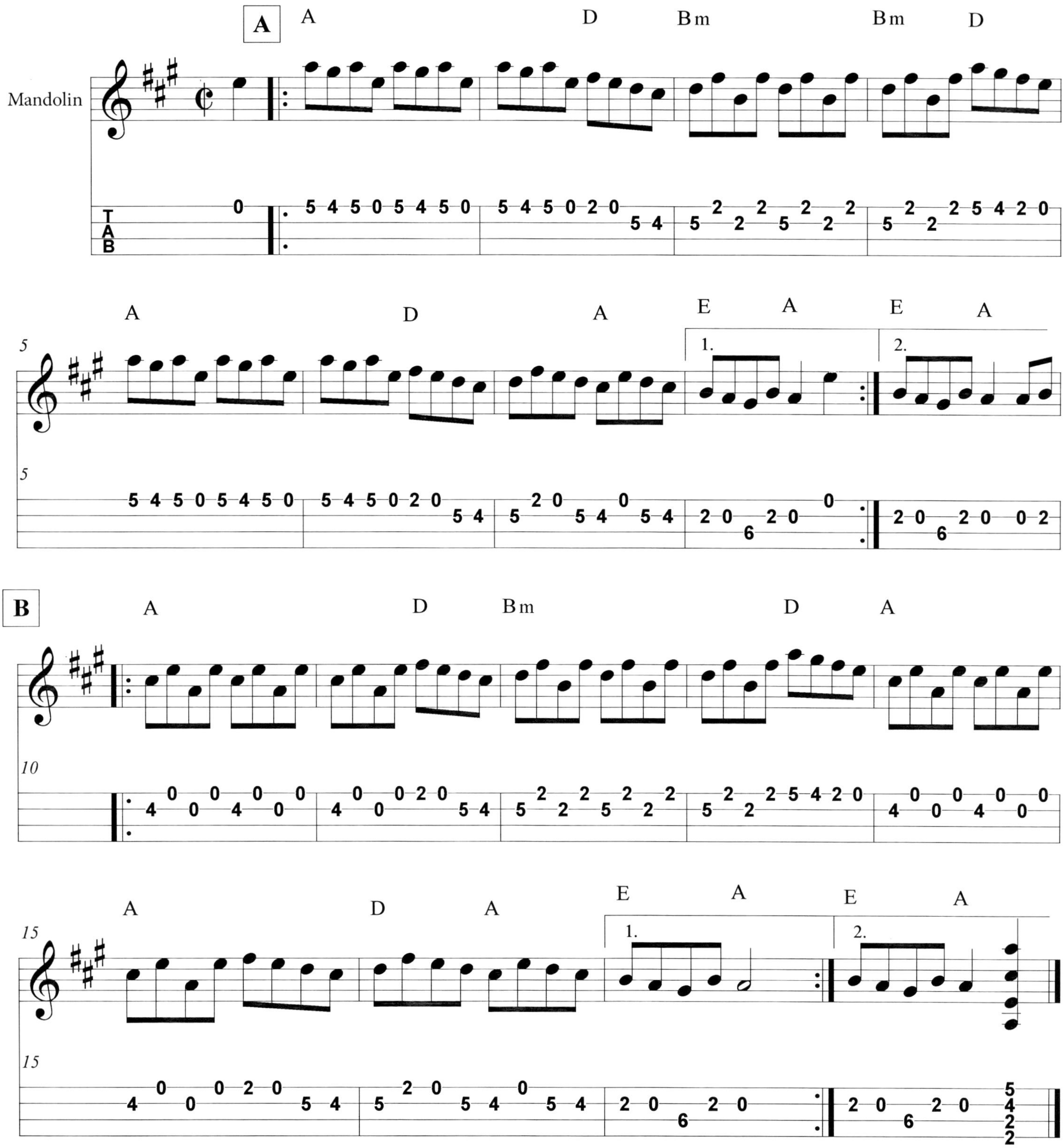

Haste to the Wedding

Haul Away, Joe

Lady's Fancy

Hens in the Kitchen

Hooker's Hornpipe

High Barbaree

Katie Trail

London Hornpipe

Maddie's Bonnet

William Bay

Dance Tempo ♩. = 108

Lonesome River

Martha's Cider

Swing Feeling ♩ = 78

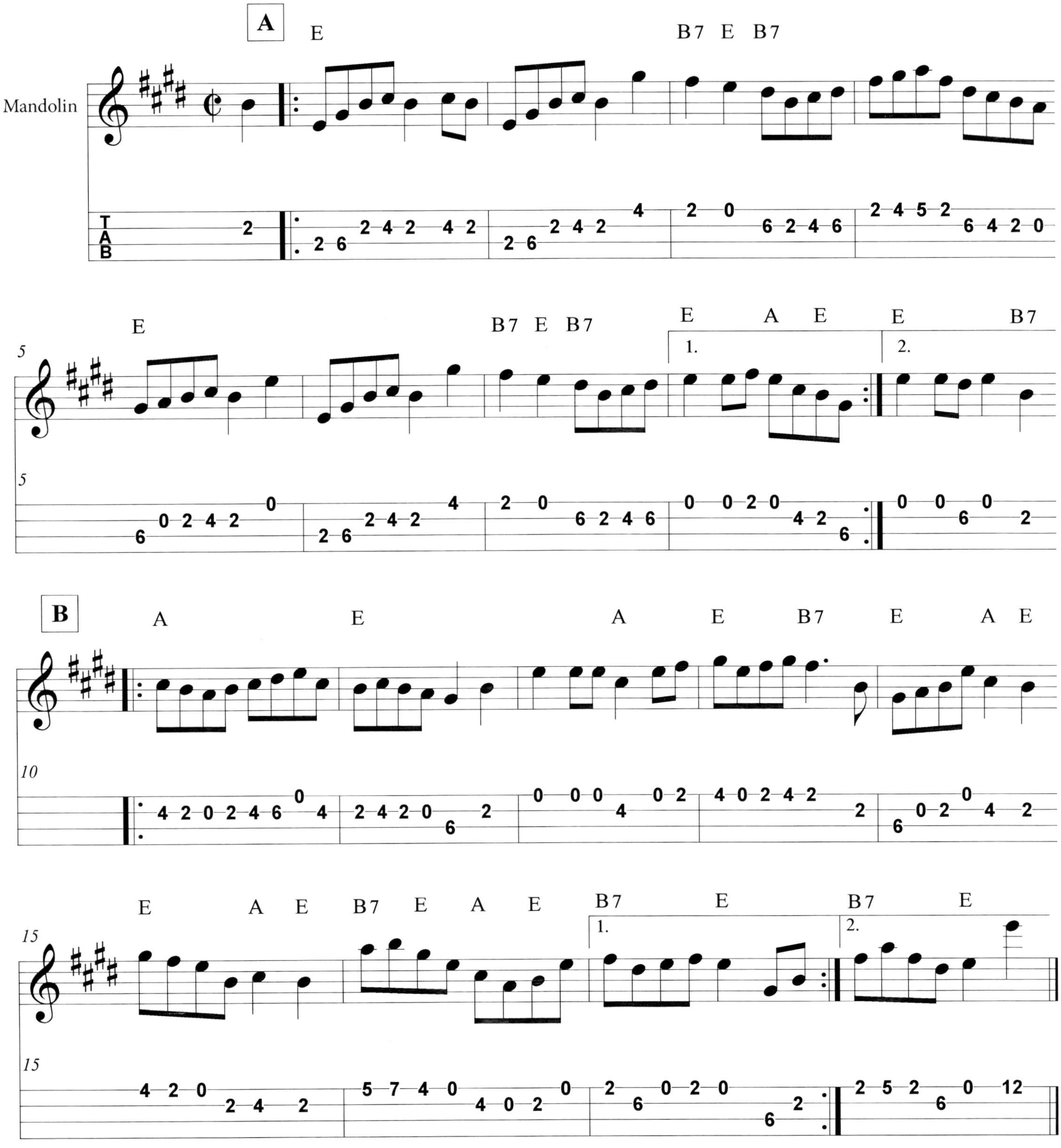

Ships are Sailing Reel

Rickett's Hornpipe

The Wild Mare

William Bay

Powder Mill

Rhythmically ♩=92

William Bay

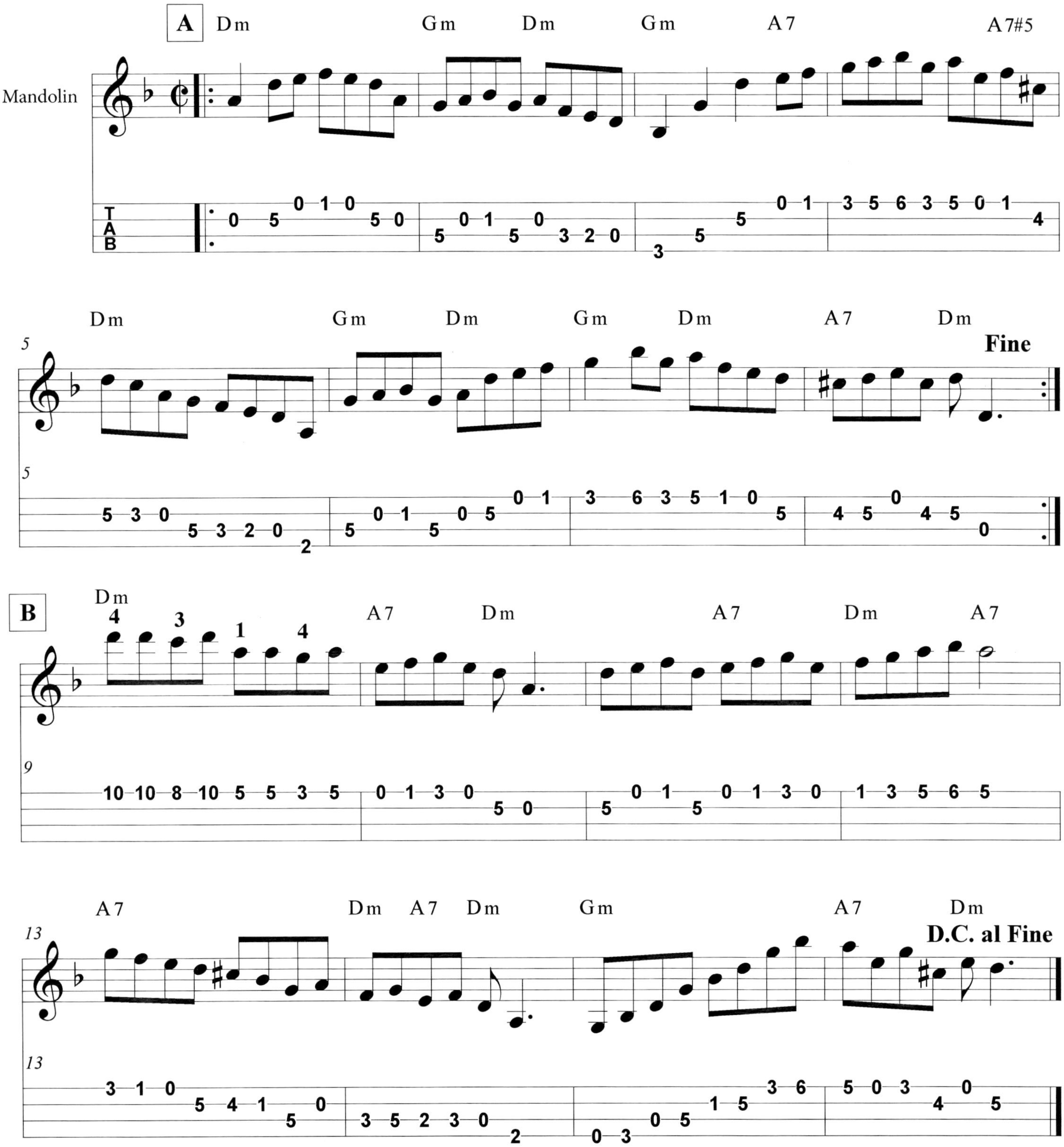

American Hornpipe

Moderately ♩=82

Other Mel Bay Mandolin Solo Books

50 Tunes for Mandolin Vol. 1 (Geslison)

101 Red Hot Bluegrass Mandolin Licks & Solos (McCabe)

All-Time Favorite Parking Lot Picker's Mandolin Solos (Bruce)

Backup Trax/Old-Time & Fiddle Tunes for Fiddle and Mandolin (Bruce)

Blazing Mandolin Solos (Kaufman)

Bluegrass Breaks: Mandolin (Bruce)

Chris Thile: Stealing Second

Classic Bluegrass Solos for Mandolin (Collins)

Complete Jethro Burns Mandolin (Burns/Eidson)

Favorite Mandolin Picking Tunes (Bruce)

Great Mandolin Picking Tunes (Carr)

Kenny Hall's Music Book: Old-Time Music for Fiddle & Mandolin (Hall/Gray)

Monroe Instrumentals: 25 Bill Monroe Favorites (Collins)

New Classics for Bluegrass Mandolin (Baldassari)

Old-Time Mandolin Solos (Eidson/Hayth)

Old-Time Stringband Workshop for Mandolin (Keefer/Weissman/Prohaska)

Old-Time Favorites for Fiddle and Mandolin (Levenson)

Old-Time Festival Tunes for Fiddle and Mandolin (Levenson)

Parking Lot Picker's Play-Along: Mandolin (Bruce)

Parking Lot Picker's Songbook (Bruce)

Shady Grove (Grisman)

Southern Mountain Mandolin (Erbsen)

Steve Kaufman's Favorite 50 Mandolin Tunes A-F

Steve Kaufman's Favorite 50 Mandolin Tunes G-M

Steve Kaufman's Favorite 50 Mandolin Tunes N-S

Steve Kaufmans Favorite 50 Mandolin Tunes S-W

String Band Classics for Mandolin (Bruce)

Texas Fiddle Favorites for Mandolin (Carr)

The Mike Marshall Collection

Tone Poems for Mandolin (Grisman)

WWW.MELBAY.COM